HONEST
Conversations

HONEST *Conversations*

IMPORTANT QUESTIONS AMERICANS SHOULD ASK THEIR FINANCIAL
ADVISOR TO HAVE MORE PRODUCTIVE CONVERSATIONS

DAN ROSENBERG

Printed in the United States of America

ISBN eBook: 978-0-9831748-1-3
ISBN Paperback: 978-0-9831748-3-7

Cover and Interior Design: Creative Publishing Book Design

Contents

Why Write this Book?

Because retail investors are asking their Financial Advisors the wrong questions!

In a dynamic world where retail investors often grapple with uncertainties, it's crucial they ask the right questions of their Financial Advisors. Gone are the days when affluent individuals solely relied on a Stockbroker's recommendation to buy individual securities. Back then, brokers earned commissions from stock sales and incentives from the companies whose stocks they sold. Mutual funds were scarcely known, and ETFs were nonexistent.

Today, the investment landscape has transformed dramatically. However, not all advisors have adapted to these changes, and many clients remain unaware of the full spectrum of value their Financial Advisors can offer.

This book is born out of my profound respect for professional money managers and security analysts. Having the privilege to learn from and collaborate with some of the most esteemed and seasoned professionals in investment management, I've gained invaluable insights. This book aims to bridge the gap between clients and advisors, equipping investors with the knowledge to ask impactful questions and make informed decisions. It's an essential guide for anyone looking to navigate the complex world of investments with confidence and clarity, and important for Americans striving for financial independence.

It still amazes me the hard work, diligence, and skill it takes to process the amount of information that professional analysts and money managers do every day. Their aptitude and diligence allow them to make billion-dollar decisions. In many cases, these individuals graduated top in their class from elite business or engineering schools, competed to earn an internship or entry-level position at an investment management firm, and then worked 12–15-hour days to become a **Junior Analyst**. They must spend another 3-5 years doing the same thing to further their career but with more pressure in a very competitive environment to become an analyst. Then, if they survive and want to continue down this career path, they have a chance to earn the role of **Lead Analyst**. In most cases, a Lead Analyst is only assigned 2-3 names to cover, and their reputation is on the line for every opinion they share and recommendation they make. Why? Because they must know EVERYTHING about these companies, from irregularities in the financial statement's footnotes to the management teams to how competitive they are in the marketplace. Then, if they prove themselves, survive the competition, and earn their CFA membership, they may have the opportunity to become a **Portfolio Manager** responsible for managing billions of dollars.

In direct contrast to this is the Financial Advisor who has none of this training, earned none of these positions, and spends three days a week on the golf course, but he seems to have a "knack" for picking securities and managing money for his clients.

After 35 years in the financial services industry (family business for almost 70), I am amazed how many clients continue to ask their financial advisor irrelevant questions like, *"What's happening in the marketplace or the economy, or what do you think about a specific security?"* These questions are irrelevant and counterproductive to your planning. Honest Conversations is designed to help retail investors have more productive conversations with their advisers and address relevant topics which can add the most value during their planning sessions. In addition, I picked out a few topics to help Americans become more financially independent, and which should be addressed with your advisor (e.g., Roth IRA's, guaranteed income for life annuities, long-term care insurance, the infinity bank concept, and the advantages of working with an RIA over a brokerage firm). These conversations lead to taking control of your finances and self-sufficiency.

The advisor's role in helping you become self-sufficient is more important than ever, but what they are supposed to be doing for you is misunderstood by the public. Through the process of building products and distribution for investment managers, I have worked with and sat across the table from tens of thousands of Financial Advisors, brokers, planners, trust officers, analysts, and money managers. So many, in fact, the number is unfathomable. I have watched many of the most successful advisors in the industry work with clients and have had the privilege to teach at training programs for some of the largest investment firms in the world. In addition, I have coached dozens of successful advisors on developing and delivering their **Value Propositions**. In each case, they are appreciative of having developed a clearly defined message that focuses on their true value of building an infrastructure to accomplish their client's planning goals *and providing niche resources to protect their client's wealth*. After completing the process of developing their value proposition, very few advisors include market commentary. In fact, it is rare to meet a Financial Advisor with the skills or background to conduct due diligence in analyzing a security. Even if I consider the hundreds of **Chartered Financial Analysts (CFAs)** who have become Financial Advisors and are qualified to conduct as well as understand research, they are way too busy managing client relationships and conducting portfolio reviews to do research. In the advisor role, they are overwhelmed by preparing for and conducting client meetings. They don't have an additional 70-80 hours per week to do their old jobs!

If a professional money manager with the **CFA**, a professional economist with a **PhD**, or a licensed equity research analyst (series 86/87) cannot predict the future, has a 50% chance of accurately guessing the next Federal Reserve or broad equity market move, why would you listen to a financial advisor who does not have the education, training, or skill set to adequately answer these questions? Think about the questions you are asking them to make your conversations more productive. The only information a client is going to receive by asking these questions is the opinion of a person who just read the market commentary or a newsletter on a website! Go to a search engine and do it yourself! Your Financial Advisor is probably not qualified to give an opinion on the market or an individual security!

So, **what conversations should you have with your Financial Advisor?** The answer is simple: to know their client's goals, liabilities, assets, income needs, risk tolerance, and generational wealth options, so together you can build a plan to accomplish specific goals. Your advisor should be able to cultivate relationships with other professionals who can add value through specific expertise for your clients and focus on the four things you can control: Risk Management, Wealth Accumulation, Wealth Distribution, and the Transfer of Wealth.

CHAPTER 1

The Origin of Information

Your Financial Advisor probably does not have any original investment ideas, nor the time or skill to conduct research to provide you with valid insight into the broad equity or fixed-income marketplace… so *DON'T* ask!

When you ask your Financial Advisor what is going on in the market? Where do they get the information from? The answer is a website or newsletter, or if they work for a large brokerage firm, they go to their website and summarize what they find in a conversation with you. The advisor has no idea what's going on except for what they read because they are probably not professional analysts. In most cases, there are only a few professionals who are qualified to conduct analysis or interpret research, and they are a **Chartered Financial Analyst (CFA)**, a professional **Equity Research Analyst** (FINRA series 86,87), or maybe a **PhD** in economics/finance/engineering.

There are exceptions, of course, as elite business and engineering schools produce their fair share of money managers. In fairness, they usually end up becoming CFA's.

So, let's briefly go through what the day in the life of an equity research analyst looks like. These professionals research public companies and come up with recommendations for their institutions about whether to buy, sell, or continue holding certain securities. Analysts are usually assigned to a particular group of companies in a specific industry for which they are responsible. Brokerage firms are known as *sell-side* if they provide research, and their customers employ equity research analysts. Mutual funds, hedge funds, and other investment firms that manage clients' money and invest on their behalf, known as the *buy side*, also employ equity research analysts to make recommendations to their portfolio managers.

Equity research analysts get an early start on the day before the market opens to keep abreast of what's going on with the 2-3 companies they cover. They do this by keeping up with wire services and other news sources and tracking global economic and market developments as well as technical trends all day. They will stay on top of any breaking news impacting the stock market and the companies they cover, receiving input from industry-specific and general news sources.

Equity research analysts must also inform and update colleagues on the sales side with recommendations and insight on various stocks so brokers can better explain those choices to clients. This requires critical and creative thinking, as well as the ability to synthesize data quickly and accurately from several different sources to present that information clearly and concisely. They work 12-15 hours per day! Equity research analysts need to be able to anticipate and prepare their sales side colleagues about the securities they cover and update senior analysts and portfolio managers about actions taken on the securities they cover.

In addition, equity research analysts come up with forecasts, earnings estimates, and opinions on how the companies they cover have performed during earnings season, as well as updating their earnings models for these companies. They also must track any developments that could affect the stock value of any of the companies they follow. They work 12-15 hours per day! Also, equity research analysts meet with the management teams of the companies they cover to get the most timely information to update the earnings estimates reports while management provides information to the analyst. They must go to the home offices to **feel the dirt!** *They have to be careful not to share any information that might impact the company's stock price and isn't available to the public, which would be illegal.*

The Securities and Exchange Commission issued rules relating to such fair disclosure practices, meaning analysts must tread carefully with management. Some companies tend not to cooperate with analysts they feel have not treated them fairly on their reports. Analysts need to provide investors with an accurate picture of a company's potential, but they also don't want to alienate a company's management and risk losing access to important information.

There are FINRA regulations for professionals who are qualified to conduct research & perform due diligence. This information is taken directly from their website, so you understand how important it is!

FINRA Rule 2241: *Research, Analysts, and Research Reports*: This rule governs conflicts of interest in connection with the publication of equity research reports and public appearances by research analysts. The rule requires firms to establish and implement policies and procedures to identify and manage research-related conflicts of interest. Among other things, policies must separate research from investment banking with respect to the supervision of research analysis, budget determinations, and compensation of analysts. The rule further prohibits promises of favorable research and analyst participation in the solicitation of investment banking businesses and road shows. The rule also requires disclosure of investment banking and other material conflicts of interest, such as personal and firm ownership of a subject company's securities.

FINRA Rule 2242: *Debt Research Analysts and Debt Research Reports*: This rule governs conflicts of interest in connection with the publication of debt research reports and the public appearances by debt research analysts. The rule imposes requirements similar to Rule 2241 on debt research distributed to retail investors, with some modifications to reflect the unique nature of the debt markets. The rule specifies the prohibited and permissible interactions between the debt research personnel and the sales and trading and principal trading personnel. The rule also exempts from many of its provisions and all of the specific disclosure requirements of debt research that is distributed only to eligible institutional investors.

FINRA Rule: 1220(b)(6): *Research Analysts:* These rules require equity research analysts to be registered with FINRA and pass a qualification examination to obtain a waiver. The Series 86/87-Research Analysts Qualification Examination (RS) assesses the competency of an entry-level equity research analyst candidate to perform the critical job functions as a research analyst, including preparing and analyzing equity securities or individual companies and industry sector research reports. They work 12-15 hours per day! There currently is no equivalent requirement for debt research analysts.

Now that you know what a real **equity research analyst** does for a living, it becomes obvious that your local Financial Advisor cannot do any of these things! Even if they were an equity research analyst or Chartered Financial Analyst (**CFA**) previously, now that they have become an advisor or work with an advisory team, they will be the first to share with you that they do not have an extra 60 to 80 hours per week to conduct original research and the due diligence on individual securities.

Therefore, do not ask your Financial Advisor what is happening in the market because they have no idea, and it is irrelevant to your planning!

VALUABLE QUESTIONS TO ASK YOUR FINANCIAL ADVISOR

- What do you like about my money manager, and why did you choose them to manage my wealth?

- Is this money manager accomplishing *my goals* based on *my risk tolerance* and *time horizon*?

CHAPTER 2

The Due Diligence Process Creates a Reversion to the Mean for Product Offerings

We are all selling the same stuff!

Do *not* believe for a minute your Financial Advisor can offer you any type of differentiating products if they are part of a broker-dealer, TAMP, trust company, or bank. *They are not allowed to sell or offer you any type of investment product that has not been through the company's due diligence process.* The due diligence process at a broker-dealer, bank, TAMP, or trust company is designed to eliminate any type of unforeseen risk (corporate or investment process) or the potential blowup of a product. These organizations are not willing to allow a product on their platform that does not meet stringent corporate and risk management criteria. I have worked with the due diligence teams from almost every brokerage firm, bank, and TAMP, and they all look at very similar types of risk based on the corporation and then the investment process. They review corporate structure, governance, stability management, FINRA, SEC, background checks, and a host of other things. Then, they look at the history of product offerings, risk metrics, process, attribution, and the money manager's distribution capacity to support the firm. In most cases, you cannot begin the due diligence process or even think about getting a product on a platform unless the performance has been audited by a 3rd party and is **GIPS** (Global Investment Performance Standard) compliant. For all you self-proclaimed money managers, this process goes trade by trade, so there is no place to hide or exceptions for bad trades! I have seen firms go trade by trade to validate performance and to see how they held up during a correction or VIX spike. If they pass the gauntlet of due diligence, they will offer these products to the Financial Advisors who access their platform. Advisors are **only allowed to offer products on their platforms**, or they will have substantial compliance issues to deal with and could even be charged with *selling away*. Therefore, almost every Financial Advisor ends up selling a very similar type of product. *This is a good thing; it is designed to protect the retail public from undue risk.*

CHAPTER 3

The Conversations You Should Be Having with Your Financial Advisor

Building a Plan to protect and transfer your wealth, create financial independence, and utilizing other professionals and niche experts to create a winning wealth management team.

Great Financial Advisors are facilitators of relationships! There are dozens of things a good Financial Advisor should do for you, but the process is quite uniform in the end. Which parts of the process get implemented depends on your specific needs? It is a team effort between you and the advisor.

There are only four things a Financial Advisor can do for you, your family, and your business:
1) Risk Management
2) Accumulate Wealth
3) Distribute Wealth
4) Transfer Wealth

A good advisor can address all these needs, goals, and ideas during planning. As the relationship grows and systems are put in place, you will have the basis to address each new change in your life.

Risk Management

- **The Business**: Succession Planning, Buy-Sell Arrangements, Deferred Compensation Plans to retain and attract key employees, Business/Professional and Commercial Liability insurance, Errors & Omissions, Directors and Officers, and Worker's Compensation, etc. The idea is that your advisor talks to you about all of these topics and introduces you to a professional on their team who can add expertise.

- **The Family**: life insurance, health insurance, disability insurance, personal liability protection, long-term care insurance, homeowners' insurance, auto insurance, insurance for artwork, jewelry, yachts, etc.

Accumulate Wealth

Ultimately, you will not become wealthy by investing in packaged products (mutual funds, ETFs, Annuities, brokerage accounts, etc.). People accrue wealth through their careers, direct investments, stock options, or inheriting wealth. Successful people will always earn more building or selling their businesses than they will through a brokerage account. There are exceptions, and I can provide dozens of examples where retail investors got lucky with tech stock or a hot dot.com. Most wealth comes from selling a business, stock in a business, or selling a real asset or intellectual property (real estate, patent, etc.). Therefore, manage expectations of what your Financial Advisor can do for you with the tools he has at his disposal. Consider an RIA as they may have more flexibility regarding product breadth (e.g., start-ups or seed-level capital opportunities) than a broker at a broker-dealer.

Distribute Wealth

This is "NOT" intended to be tax advice; it is just conversations you should be having with your Financial Advisor! Seek help from a tax professional before you make any decisions!

Withdraw from taxable accounts first:

Non-qualified or taxable accounts are those that are not tax-advantaged and include checking and savings accounts, standard or joint brokerage accounts, and employer stock purchase plans. Taxable brokerage accounts are your least tax-efficient accounts, subject to capital gains and dividend taxes. Using these funds first in retirement gives your tax-advantaged accounts (IRA, Roth IRA) more time to grow and compound. Taxable accounts will never grow as quickly as tax-advantaged accounts because they are subject to the annual drag of taxation on interest, dividends, and capital gains.

Withdraw from Tax-Deferred Accounts Second:

These are the traditional IRA, 401(k), 403(b), and annuities. All of which are subject to ordinary income tax rates when you withdraw money from them. One reason you withdraw from tax-deferred accounts is that you'll know roughly what tax rates are going to be in the short term. Those rates are relatively low now; the 2017 Tax Cuts and Jobs Act expires at the end of 2025. From a tax perspective, it doesn't matter whether you start withdrawing first from a traditional IRA or 401(k), but keep in mind that required minimum distributions (RMDs) for both accounts begin in the year you turn age 73.

Withdraw from Roth IRAs, Roth 401(k)'s Last:

A prudent retirement income and tax strategy maximize tax-advantaged growth while maintaining the flexibility of funding some portion of your retirement expenses with non-taxable income. If it makes sense for your situation, a Roth Conversion Strategy in which you convert portions of tax-deferred accounts to a Roth account may add tremendous value in tax-free distribution, avoiding RMDs or transferring wealth to an heir.

Transfer Wealth

The Estate Planning Documents to Protect Your Family: Pre-need Guardian Designations, Advanced Health Care Directive, Letter of Intent, Beneficiary Designations, List of Important Documents (accessible during emergencies), Provision of Digital Assets, Durable Power of Attorney, Revocable Living Trust, Living Will, Last Will & Testament, Durable Powers of Attorney for medical and financial, Revocable Living Trust, Last Will & Testament.

A good advisor will address and discuss the risks you face personally and professionally. Do you have life insurance to protect your family and address your estate tax liability? Distribute your accumulated wealth based on income goals, tax consequences, and wealth transfer opportunities. Your Financial Advisor or accountant should map out a tax-smart distribution strategy.

This is another example of the value of your Financial Advisor's network of professionals. If they introduced you to an Estate Planning attorney to design the proper documents, kudos to your Financial Advisor! Baby Boomers have $30 Trillion to pass down to their millennial heirs, who are largely skeptical of financial services professionals and the industry in general. They don't trust Wall Street and believe they can do it themselves with digital tools. While there are some truths to both, dozens of decisions must be made to properly transfer this wealth, preserve it from taxes, and avoid going to probate. If you want assets to go to the intended people and to be used as the parents attended, as well as protect children in the event of divorce or a health issue, you need a good Financial Advisor with a robust team to support them. Tax-efficient planning for generational wealth should be part of every plan. Get the kids involved as early as possible with your Financial Advisor so there is a relationship in place. Have a basic understanding of what is important to you and how they're going to handle the transfer of wealth. If you're comfortable getting into details, consider sharing the types of assets you'll leave and how you would like them to be divided. Often, it is not the money that causes family fighting; it's the sentimental assets, such as a vacation home or a piece of art or jewelry. You should also be aware that your children's spouses may get involved and try to influence their expectations. So, be clear about who should be included in this conversation. Most heirs who inherit an IRA take it as a lump sum and blow it within nine months. This is why it is a good idea to talk about multi-generational IRAs, ensuring your children appreciate and understand the advantages of keeping the tax deferral throughout their lifetime. There are almost no traditional pension plans anymore, so this strategy can legally force them to stretch out the money and may provide a lifetime income stream.

After all debts have been settled, it is up to the executor or the successor trustee to distribute the assets to heirs based on your will. Therefore, make sure you have a competent decision-maker who can deal with the supporting family members who feel slighted and who would take legal action, which destroys all the wealth they were supposed to have transferred to them. It should be a well-liked, respected, persistent, and business-minded individual as this is a large responsibility. This person will have a fiduciary responsibility to follow your wishes as they are stated.

Healthcare documents need to be in order! Tell them specifically what you want to happen and have that conversation with them all at the same time. This is where we can see fights. For example, one child wants to hold on and keep a parent on a respirator or feeding tube, but no one is sure what that parent really wants because she told each sibling something different. Get ready for battle! Make sure your wishes are well-documented, and work with your estate-planning attorney so you are clear in your estate documents.

Be specific in your wishes for your heirs. The last thing you want is for some or all the money you leave to your children or grandchildren to go to a potential ex-son-in-law or ex-daughter-in-law, or for it to be lost because of a future legal issue. Proper estate planning can prevent much of this by establishing different kinds of trusts, providing clear documentation regarding any gifting, and keeping property correctly titled.

It all starts with communication with your loved ones and your team of financial professionals. Everyone should understand who's getting what, how, when, and why. You can do this with a conference call or a virtual meeting! Communicate with your Financial Advisor so he can plan to get the entire family on the same page.

I just spent time explaining the basics of wealth management, because there is a tremendous breadth and depth of services to provide for your clients that don't involve trying to be a money manager.

The Self-Unaware Money Manager:
(Everyone Outperforms the Market
until they must validate their Performance)

I cannot begin to count the advisors who believe they have some type of "Knack" or "Unique Awareness" about what is going on in the marketplace. Thousands of advisors and lots of newbies in the industry believe their value is stock picking without having the background, training, education, or experience to be either a research analyst or a professional money manager (**CFA**). They just always seem to outperform the market! However, there is a litmus test on performance metrics in the investment management industry called **GIPS** (Global Investment Performance Standards), which is a process of performance validation. It is to the Investment Management industry what **GAAP** (Generally Accepted Accounting Principles) is to the accounting industry. In other words, the advisors who claim "benchmark outperformance" and do not have their performance validated are selling you something or are self-unaware. If they could consistently outperform a benchmark, every money management firm in the world would hire them and pay them more than they make as an advisor.

So, let's just talk about some of the areas in which Financial Advisors/planners can add real value:

- Cash Flow Planning
- Succession Planning
- Charitable & Estate Planning

- Long-Term Care
- Bill Pay and Budgeting
- Next Gen Education Workshops
- Analyzing Benefit Packages
- Retirement Income Planning/Roth IRA Conversions
- Art Appraisal
- Gifting Strategies
- Risk Management, personally and professionally
- Social Security Maximization
- Unemployment Planning
- Liability protection for your family & business
- Goal Planning personally and professionally
- SLAT's

This is not an all-inclusive list, so the point is that there is enough to do and ways to add value without your advisor pretending to be a portfolio manager.

VALUABLE QUESTIONS TO ASK YOUR FINANCIAL ADVISOR

- Do I have a comprehensive financial plan to meet my goals?

- Are there any gaps in my risk management?

- Does the growth of my wealth meet my goals based on my risk tolerance and time horizon?

- Is the order of distribution from my assets efficient, and are there any changes you would make?

- Explain to me the process of how my assets will be distributed to my heirs, and are there any changes you would make?

CHAPTER 4

Actual Returns vs. Average Annual Returns

This is where the power of ZERO becomes your hero, and the Turtle wins the race. A good website to calculate is http://moneychimp.com/features/market_cagr.htm.

Stock market indexes, mutual funds, ETFs, and other investments share their performance by using **average annual returns** over a given period. One year, three years, five years, and a lifetime. They post this information on fact sheets and websites and share it with investment management reporting media. It is what most Financial Advisors provide and discuss with their clients about managing expectations. This may be factually true but is very misleading because of the *life-altering damage that drawdowns and corrections cause during the distribution phase of retirement planning.* The Actual Returns, regardless of the average annual returns, are far more important once you enter retirement and begin taking distributions. Taking distributions from your retirement plan during a drawdown or correction in the market may change your lifestyle irreparably! However, there is a way to get a 0% return during every down-market year! Let's go through a simplistic example together:

	FIA	Brokerage Account
Investment	$100,000.00	$100,000.00
Market Correction	-50%	-50%
Account Value	$100,000.00	$50,000.00
Market Rebound	+50%	+50%
Account Value	$150,000.00	$75,000.00
Annual Fees	$0.00	-$750.00 @ 1%

Let's go through this example again now that the FIA (Fixed Indexed Annuity) only earns ½ as much as the brokerage account!

	FIA	Brokerage Account
Investment	$100,000.00	$100,000.00
Market Correction	-50%	-50%
Account Value	$100,000.00	$50,000.00
Market Rebound	+25%	+50%
Account Value	$125,000.00	$75,000.00
Annual Fees	$0.00	-$750.00 @ 1%

The Average Annual Return is 0%. The Actual Return is a 25% loss (in addition to the Advisor's Fees)!

Now you see my point! Once again, ZERO is your hero, so you may consider including an FIA (Fixed Indexed Annuity) as part of your retirement income planning.

If this is the cure for cancer, political stability, for the elimination of hunger? Probably not, but if this is your largest asset and you must protect it to maintain your standard of living during retirement, it will be just as valuable to you!

A drawdown or correction when you are retiring can destroy decades of planning, or worse, if you have a health issue to deal with. It can become life-altering in a bad way. That is why 0% during a down market year is your portfolio's most important performance number. Never losing money may be the single most important factor in preserving your retirement income. The Principal Guarantee through a Fixed Indexed Annuity (FIA) can be invaluable! Eliminating downside risk is liberating and life-altering in a good way!

VALUABLE QUESTIONS TO ASK
YOUR FINANCIAL ADVISOR

- What part of my portfolio has the Principal Guaranteed against market loss?

- As I am nearing retirement, does my money manager adjust my portfolio to more conservative investments to protect my principal?

- Based on my portfolio strategy today, how would a market correction affect my retirement plan?

CHAPTER 5

The Misunderstood Annuity

The single most misunderstood investment vehicle is The Annuity. Brokerage and Investment firms use negative attack ads to malign them. Insurance companies praise them. So, what is the truth? *Considering the condition of the Social Security Trust Fund, this is a very important conversation to have with your Financial Advisor because it is one of the last investment opportunities where you can guarantee a lifetime income stream!*

An annuity is just a tool in a toolbox! Nothing more and nothing less! Remove the emotion and take a moment to understand what they can do for you, how they are built and priced, and how they manage risk. In addition, the FIAs are evolving through two primary trends which are structurally and the participation of institutional money managers. Structurally, the newer products offer upside potential with no fees, uncapped index participation, and no spreads. Secondly, the largest institutional money managers are now managing the uncapped index options (e.g., Goldman Sachs, Bank of America, Blackrock, JP Morgan, Merrill Lynch, Barclays, Credit Suisse, Dimensional, etc.). There are two primary reasons to purchase an annuity contract, guaranteed income for life and tax-deferred growth.

Guaranteed Income for Life

The only way to receive a guaranteed income for life is through a traditional pension plan, social security, an annuity, or possibly the lottery.

An annuity is a contractually guaranteed investment agreement between you and the insurance company. If you use an SPIA (single premium immediate annuity) or an FIA (fixed indexed annuity), you can receive an income stream you (and or your partner jointly) cannot outlive. For people nearing retirement, this may be a very important tool to maintain your standard of living and provide peace of mind. Having a specified amount electronically deposited into their account at the same time each month may give some people the freedom to chase their dreams, travel around the world, or spend more time with their children or grandchildren. It can be a life-changing tool in your planning process.

Protected Growth Strategy
(The Fixed Indexed Annuity as an Asset Class)

Fixed Annuities provide a guaranteed return for a specified period. **FIA's** (*Fixed Indexed Annuities*) similarly guarantee your principal against market loss and may provide an opportunity for growth. In other words, you may get some of the upside of the market or index you invest in, with no downside risk of loss! This type of attribution may even be valuable as a bond complement, a fixed-income substitute, or a non-correlated asset class in a portfolio. In many ways, it behaves as a unique asset class which may mitigate portfolio risk. In addition, you can create this Protected Growth Strategy with no fees, caps, costs, or expenses and institutional money management. This is why brokerage firms and money managers hate these products because they simply cannot compete!

So, if an **FIA** (fixed indexed annuity) may be able to outpace inflation, provide growth, and have no downside risk, how can the insurance company afford to underwrite this type of contract?

- Interest Earned on Fixed Income Investments from the premiums paid
- Surrender Charges
- Options on the indexes
- Fees on the Benefit Riders (e.g., Living Benefits, Death Benefits, LTC, etc).

While caps, fees, spreads, and participation rates have become optional on most contracts, the surrender charge forces the annuitant to stay in the contract long enough for the insurance company to make enough profit to cover its liability. In addition, if you invest in strategies with caps, spreads, or participation rates, they will take some of the upside of your growth. Is this a bad thing? *Heck No!* You have the potential for Guaranteed Income for Life, access to 5%-10% of your assets through the penalty-free withdrawal feature, potential growth to outpace inflation, no fees, costs, or expenses, and no loss of principal! This is one of the best tools in your toolbox for retirement planning!

There is no risk to your principal; it is guaranteed by the full strength of the issuing insurance company; while a CD is FDIC insured up to a certain amount, the Legal Reserve requirements of the insurance company make sure your insurer is financially solvent and strong enough to withstand just about anything. If you have doubts, look at what happened during the Great Depression. The financial reliability of the life insurance industry was demonstrated convincingly during the Great Depression of 1929-38. Approximately 9,000 banks suspended operations, while 99% of all life insurance in force continued unaffected. Reinsurance, acquisitions, and mergers protected virtually all policy owners in the affected companies against personal loss.

VALUABLE QUESTIONS TO ASK YOUR FINANCIAL ADVISOR

- Is my principal protected against market loss?

- What are all my contract's fees, costs, and expenses?

- What are the surrender charges and penalties if I cancel the contract?

- What are the caps, spreads, and participation rates of the index I am investing in?

- Does this contract offer an index option with no caps or fees?

- Is my income contractually guaranteed for my or joint lifetime?

- What is my annual liquidity amount without any penalty?

CHAPTER 6

The Rise of the RIA

If you want a Financial Advisor who will put your goals and needs ahead of his own firm and deferred compensation plan, find an RIA.

Broker-dealers are regulated by the Financial Industry Regulatory Authority (**FINRA**) and must meet specific requirements. For example, they must have adequate capital and sound business practices to protect investors.

Registered investment advisory professionals advise individuals, institutions, and other organizations on investments and financial planning. Registered investment advisors must register either their state or the Securities and Exchange Commission (**SEC**). Depending on the type of assets to manage, they must provide ongoing reporting to ensure compliance with state and federal laws and regulations.

In practice, there's a huge difference in how employees of broker-dealers behave and get compensated, versus the independence of a registered investment advisor. Employees of broker-dealers have compensation packages based on the assets they manage, cross-product marketing, and meeting minimum production requirements. These deferred compensation arrangements are based on corporate designed production requirements. In addition, they may receive enormous bonuses with a multiple of their trailing revenue, by moving their books of business from one broker-dealer to another.

Independent registered investment advisors get paid an hourly fee for planning, or from assets under management, or a combination thereof. They do not have production requirements or proprietary products to cross sell. Therefore, there is no bias or incentive to market proprietary products. Since there are no proprietary products, platforms, or market commentary to promote, the independent registered investment advisor can always could put the client first. There is no conflict of interest as all RIA's are self-employed and do not have to submit to the parent companies' perspective or way of doing business.

VALUABLE QUESTIONS TO ASK
YOUR FINANCIAL ADVISOR

- Do I have any proprietary products, and why?

- Are there any Non-Proprietary options that accomplish the same goals and have lower fees?

Infinity Bank: (Be Your Own Bank)

"It's mainstream, so let's talk about it"

The reason I am including a chapter about the Infinity Bank Concept (**IBC**), is because of the value the strategy has added to my personal planning, as well as many of the clients I have worked with. Recently, a retired public-school employee asked me about this concept, so I have to believe it is mainstream. Let's talk about it! At least in modern times, this concept was started by an economist named Nelson Nash in the 1980s (*Becoming Your Own Banker*). If you want to become more financially self-sufficient and are affluent or have cash flow that provides a tremendous amount of disposable income, utilizing a cash-value life insurance policy as a separate asset class to take tax-free loans may add value to your retirement plan. Infinity banking is a personal finance strategy that allows the use of a permanent life insurance policy as a personal line of credit. The Infinity Banking Concept (or

IBC) is the process by which one becomes one's own banker. In his book, Nash explains how whole life insurance policies uniquely function as dividend-paying assets through accrued equity. He explains several creative ways to use the liquid cash value in these policies. For example:

- Creating your own tax-free lending system to finance large purchases (i.e., a car or a home) independently of commercial banks and lenders.
- Generating personal wealth without the volatility of equities and with the added utility of naming a beneficiary to transfer the wealth outside of probate if done properly.
- Using these practices for business financing
- Repay cash flow and liquidity to the policy to create continuous compounding.

Whole life cash value guarantees a specific rate of return through a dividend at the end of the policy year, and Index universal life policies are credited an interest rate at the end of every year. Once you've accumulated enough cash value, you can begin to borrow against your policy. The infinite part of infinity banking refers to the life policy insurance payout when you die. Since whole life insurance policies always pay, a person can continue the infinite banking strategy through policy loans throughout their life and create multi-generational wealth. Infinity banking has been used by wealthy families and large corporations to build generational wealth for a very long time. Moderately wealthy people can utilize this strategy through enhanced policy designs of the IUL (indexed Universal Life) contracts.

VALUABLE QUESTIONS TO ASK
YOUR FINANCIAL ADVISOR

- Based on the Guaranteed Rates in the contract, how much Cash Surrender Value will I have access to in 5,10, 15, and 20 years from now, to take as a loan from the contract?

- What are all the costs, fees, and expenses in my contract?

- How much of my premiums is put into the savings portion of my contract, and how much is deducted for costs, fees, and expenses?

- Do the amount of my costs, fees, and expenses change over time, and by how much?

CHAPTER 8

Roth IRA Conversions That Someone Else Pays For?

How will you be affected when the Tax Cuts and Job Act (TCJA) sunsets in 2025? Converting pretax savings to a Roth IRA may make sense in some situations. Where the amount converted will be taxable and recognized as ordinary income, a preferred strategy may be to convert part of your savings each year. If structured properly, a partial Roth IRA conversion may help you avoid getting pushed into a higher tax bracket, and there are insurance companies which have products who offer accumulation bonuses to offset some of this tax liability.

A partial or full Roth conversion may provide you with tax-free growth, qualified distributions may be income tax-free, there are no required minimum distributions, no income eligibility limits, and legacy distributions may be income tax-free. A systematic decrease of your pretax IRA and increase into a Roth IRA, if done properly, may be able to maintain your current tax rate.

Some states partially or totally exclude retirement income from state income taxes, which might mitigate the value of the Roth IRA conversion. Take the time to discuss this with your local Financial Advisor and tax professional.

If you do a partial Roth IRA conversion, there is a five-year waiting period before you can distribute the converted Roth IRA accounts without owing the 10% additional tax. Each part of the conversion starts its own five-year period. The five-year period begins on January 1st and applies to each annual conversion until you reach the age of 59 ½.

Roth IRA conversions may affect your Medicare surtax! Married couples filing jointly with modified adjusted gross income (MAGI) of more than $250,000 (2023 limits) may be subject to a 3.8% Medicare surtax. Be aware that income from the conversion may put you over the MAGI limit, consequently affecting whether the tax advantage was beneficial.

Some of the new annuity products on the marketplace provide bonuses to pay some of your tax liability from the conversion. The evolution of these fixed-indexed annuities (FIAs) is quite interesting. They may be able to help you convert your traditional IRA into a Roth IRA with limited money out of your pocket! You may consider this type of strategy during the distribution phase of your retirement plan and talk to your Financial Advisor, as well as your tax planning professional, to help you make the best decision. Money in Roth IRAs or Roth 401(k)s is not taxable income when you withdraw from them if you follow the rules (e.g., must be 59½ or older and have held the account for at least five years). Withdrawals are tax-free for your heirs regardless of their age, if the original account was opened at least five years before.

The idea for the account holder is to let it sit and grow tax-free as long as possible before tapping into it. There is no RMD for a Roth IRA account holder, although there is one for the Roth 401(k) and those inheriting Roths. When you convert a traditional IRA or 401(k) to a Roth IRA, you will be taxed at your ordinary tax rate for that year on the amount you converted. There is no limit on the amount you can convert each year, but executing the conversion over several years usually makes sense to lessen the tax hit. Converting a large amount in one year might push you into a higher tax bracket.

When doing Roth conversions (partial or whole), it's important to consider what the funds will be invested in. Given the growth potential of a Roth, it may be a good idea to start making some annual Roth conversions from tax-deferred accounts during your buildup years toward retirement — the earlier, the better.

VALUABLE QUESTIONS TO ASK
YOUR FINANCIAL ADVISOR

- What is the most efficient time period for me to complete a Roth IRA conversion?

- Based on my tax bracket, does a Roth IRA conversion make sense for me, and what will be the taxable amount?

- What are the advantages to me and my heirs, and what is the impact on my RMDs?

- What is the best investment choice to fund my Roth IRA conversion with?

- Will a Roth IRA conversion cause any Medicare surtax, and is it relevant to my specific situation?

CHAPTER 9

You Will Need Long-Term Care Insurance!

Again, the theme here is to take control of your finances and become more self-sufficient! Anyone who turns 65 today has almost a 70% chance of needing some type of long-term care services and support in their remaining years. Women need care longer (3.7 years) than men (2.2 years). One-third of today's 65-year-olds may never need long-term care support, but 20 percent will need it for longer than five years. Only about 7.5 million Americans, or 3.3% of the population, own long-term care insurance. Most Americans are unprepared for long-term care cost. New research shows healthcare cost remain a top financial concern for Americans, second only to gas and transportation cost. Research suggests that Americans may be overlooking their long-term healthcare needs and associated financial health.

According to the US Department of Health and Human Services, nearly 70% of 65-year-olds will need long-term care in their lifetimes. These services include medical and personal care services at home or in a facility where people can no longer care for themselves independently. The average person will need services for three years, and 20% will need help for five years or more. Long-term care services can cost six figures per year, and recent surveys suggest that many middle-income adults will be unprepared for those costs.

A recent survey was conducted by **HCG Secure** in partnership with the **Arctos Foundation** and included approximately 400 adults between the ages of 40 and 64 whose annual household income was between $75,000 and $150,000.

Half of respondents said they or their partner will need long-term care services, but only one-quarter have or are considering getting long-term care insurance or a savings account for long-term care expenses.

Most people aren't even talking about long-term care at all. More than half (57%) haven't discussed their long-term care needs and preferences with their family or friends. This lack of open dialogue concerns planners trying to protect their clients.

Everyone should be having conversations with family about how they want to be treated and the care delivered in the event they require long-term care coverage. Most people should be earmarking a significant portion of personal savings for long-term care needs or purchasing a lower-cost policy to cover some expenses arising from a minimum of one year of long-term care needs.

It is always better to do something rather than nothing, and this survey shows that very few Americans are prepared for this liability.

When asked how they expect to pay for future long-term care services, 54% of survey respondents said they will use their own savings. This figure was higher among people without a college degree (59%). Only 22% expect to receive financial support from long-term care insurance. 41% expect financial support from government insurance. However, most people cannot get everything they need from government-sponsored insurance.

Medicare, health insurance primarily for Americans 65 and older, covers some nursing home and rehab facility costs (up to 100 days) and some home health care expenses. It does not, however, cover the costs of assistance with activities of daily living, such as eating, bathing, toileting, or moving around. About half (51%) of people surveyed did not know that.

Medicaid, health insurance primarily for lower-income Americans, covers some long-term care expenses, including personal care services in some instances, but only for people who qualify based on income or other state-level eligibility rules. One-fifth of respondents aren't sure how they will pay for long-term care.

Not only are people unsure how they will pay for the cost of care over time, but they also aren't particularly well versed in how much it will cost. Only 7% said they were very familiar with long-term care costs, and nearly half (48%) said they did not know.

Respondents were optimistic when asked to estimate how much it would cost to cover assistance with activities of daily living. The median "best guess" for these costs was $25,000 per year.

Costs vary widely by type of service and location but typically average more. According to Genworth's 2021 cost of care data, the national median cost for one year of nursing home care ranges from about $95,000 to nearly $110,000, depending on the type of room (private or semi-private).

In the HCG Secure survey, 7 out of 10 respondents said they want to receive long-term care at home, and 10% said that's the only option they will consider. Home-based care is expensive. Genworth data show that the median annual costs for home health aides and homemakers are approximately $60,000 each.

Presented with actual average costs for long-term care, survey respondents were unpleasantly surprised. Sixty percent said the actual costs are more or much more than they expected. Two-thirds said they would not be prepared to pay for in-home help with personal care. Once survey respondents understood the real costs, only 30% said they would change their long-term financial plans to be prepared. Of those, about half (53%) said they need to save more money, and 25% would consider getting different insurance coverage.

More than one-third (33%) said they feel it is unlikely that they will need some type of help with daily living in the future, and people who don't expect to need long-term care cited their good health habits and a lack of family history.

A competent Financial Advisor is so important because of the general lack of preparedness. Long-term care insurance can be expensive and difficult to get, especially for people without financial resources.

Despite a ton of research showing that most Americans will need this support with age, most people are willing to risk the financial and emotional stability of their families in the future based on their current health status. This illustrates how the current discussions around our country's long-term care crisis are not being adequately addressed. The impact on middle-income Americans and families will be substantial. *This is another example of an important conversation where your time is well spent with your Financial Advisor!* Make a plan and budget something for this liability to protect yourself and your family.

VALUABLE QUESTIONS TO ASK
YOUR FINANCIAL ADVISOR

- How will I address my LTC needs?

- Is Indemnity, Cash Indemnity, or Reimbursement the best option for my situation?

- Am I better off obtaining this coverage through a Single Premium Life Insurance contract with LTC benefits, An annuity with LTC benefits, or purchasing a Long-Term Care policy?

- What premiums and benefits are contractually guaranteed from each option?

- Will my premium increase or remain level for my lifetime? What type of premium guarantees exist in this contract?

CHAPTER 10

The CPA Trap

Every Certified Public Accountant (**CPA**) I have met or worked with is a bright and well-educated professional. They provide invaluable information on tax planning and auditing as well as broad categories of financial reporting. However, very few have any background, licensing, credentials, or training in investment management or risk management. How do I know this, because I receive referrals from CPA's who stay in their lane and focus on their areas of expertise. In addition, the best CPA's have robust relationships with specialists who can add the most value to their clients. The reason I have included this chapter in my book (your guide to more productive planning conversations) is because I have experienced the most ridiculous and borderline incompetent investment management and insurance guidance from CPA's who provide opinions outside of their training and education.

They usually are not licensed or have been through any type of investment management or analyst training program. Do not ask them about investment management or insurance because they usually do not have a background in it! The Trap is where they provide guidance in areas, they do not have expertise in, and you believe them because they are your accountant or a CPA. Do NOT fall into this trap!

What are a CPA's Primary Responsibilities and Training

CPAs can work in a variety of settings and perform numerous job duties. The specifics of their job responsibilities change depending on the company they work for, and their client's goals and objectives. Common job duties for CPAs include:

- **Tax oversight:** Many CPAs prepare and file a company's taxes. They may also represent the company in interactions with the IRS if needed.
- **Record keeping:** CPAs manage financial record keeping independently or on a team of other financial professionals.
- **Reports:** Most CPAs serve as both a financial expert and a liaison to the company's upper management team. CPAs often create financial reports and present them to company leaders.
- **Audits:** CPAs also perform internal audits of the company's finances to ensure all the recordkeeping is accurate

and hat they account for all the money that comes into the business and leaves the business.

- **Forecasts:** Some CPAs also assist their company's leadership with financial forecasting. They may provide potential quarterly or annual profit projections or help with investing capital.

- **Compliance:** CPAs help businesses ensure regulatory compliance. They also update any processes and procedures in the accounting department to reflect regulatory changes.

With this impressive skill set, a CPA may be the most trusted overall financial advisor for Americans. Rightfully so, because part of what they do may encompass not only your annual tax liability, but your personal and corporate retirement planning.

In reference to your businesses, their guidance can be substantial by properly structuring and choosing the most efficient corporate structure, as well as which retirement plans are most advantageous for your company. For most Americans, their business is their most valuable asset.

Ask your risk management or investment management specialist to work directly with your accountant or CPA. After almost 40 years of wealth management, I have rarely seen a retail investor accurately or adequately explain to their CPA how their investments or insurance products work, so *don't do it!* Ask your accountant or CPA to work with your specialists as you should be the captain of your own financial planning team. On many occasions, I have been involved with clients who received poor guidance on investment and insurance products which their accountant or CPA did not fully understand. In some cases, I have also seen CPA's give poor guidance because they do not want another advisor to build a relationship with their client. Your CPA is probably a bright and well-educated professional who can add tremendous value as part of your financial planning team. Let them stick to the areas of their expertise and utilize other professionals to help you create a more fundamentally sound financial plan.

CHAPTER 11

The Future of Wealth Management

Robo advice still can't navigate complex financial situations and is incapable of explaining nuanced planning and tax scenarios. The emotions involved in the decision-making process and providing periodic emotional reassurances that clients crave from a human advisor are still vital in the planning process.

Affluent individuals will always want human interaction and guidance from a professional who can help them and whom they trust! Technology will continue to add value in calculations and processes, but serious wealth will always require interpersonal communication. So, find an advisor who cares about you, knows how to help you, and brings a wealth of resources to your family, business, or your cause! If they pretend to be a market expert and begin talking about how their uniquely designed portfolios outperform their peers, run for the hills! Human advisors bring financial plans to life using empathy, intuition, and experience. Robo FAQs and forums are not enough! As technology changes and new asset classes emerges like Crypto, this presents more opportunities to work with your advisor, not less.

The financial services industry is continuously evolving, leading to questions about the future of Financial Advisors. The good news is that personal financial advisor growth is estimated at 15% through 2031. Rapid advancements in technology and shifting demand for advice among consumers will necessitate a new approach regarding how advisors work.

Financial services are increasingly going digital, thanks to online tools and platforms that make it easy for people to track investments and get advice without leaving home. While plenty of investors still prefer in-person meetings with their advisors, just as many opt to stay in touch via email, text, chat, or video calls.

Robo advisor platforms have emerged which may be seen as competitors to human advisor roles. While Robo-advisor technology is far from perfect, algorithms are constantly being tested and refined to offer clients a better experience and more personalized advice. Some Robo-advisors have even begun experimenting with artificial intelligence (AI) to enhance their services.

The evolution of Practice Management is increasing financial advisor efficiency, lowering fees, and being aided by incorporating technology. For example, cloud-based software programs and automation are helping advisors to work more efficiently and streamline tasks so that they're free to focus on advising clients. Financial Advisors who fail to adapt to these changes could result in being left behind.

Your advisor can also gain an edge by embracing technology that directly benefits their business through time saved, money saved, or both.

Demographics Are Shifting, and Advice is Changing

The youngest baby boomers are still a few years away from full retirement age. The future of Financial Advisors may lie with their children (Gen Xers) and grandchildren (Millennials), so your advisor needs to be prepared!

Trillions of dollars in assets are set to flow from baby boomers to the next generation through the *Great Wealth Transfer*.

This begins with relationship building for the older clients and then with their children. How your advisor goes about doing that should depend on your expectations and what you're doing to meet them. What if you are concerned about how long-term care costs might impact your heir's wealth down the line? This presents an opportunity to start a family conversation, which includes their children about how long-term care needs will be met if you cannot make decisions for yourself.

Trust is the essential element in these conversations, which good advisors seek to establish from day one. It's also important to remember the needs of future generations may not be the same as yours, and the services or advice your advisor is offering may need to be adapted to reflect that. Your advisor needs to remember what form that advice that will take, does it resonate, how it will be delivered, and the unique needs you and your family may have in the future. You control the dynamics of your own wealth management, so take control and ask more productive questions.

Advisors need to remember what form that advice will take, how it will be delivered, and what unique needs clients may have in the future. What will the client's social security benefits look like in retirement once surplus trust funds are depleted? That's still roughly a decade away, but it's something that bears consideration now.

About the Author

r. Rosenberg is a 35-year investment industry veteran with experience as a successful financial planning professional and an institutional distribution executive. In addition, he has learned best practices while sitting across the table and learning from tens of thousands of Financial Advisors. Mr. Rosenberg has helped thousands of individuals protect their wealth, their future, and their legacy. He has consulted REITs, hedge funds, insurance companies, boutique money managers, and large investment firms to create products, platforms, and the infrastructure for distribution. As regional director and national sales manager, he has been a top-tiered and award-winning producer for some of the world's largest investment and insurance companies. Mr. Rosenberg has been a presenter and coached some of the most successful Financial Advisors in the industry on public speaking and presentation skills, developing a value proposition, branding, and practice management.

Graduating with a Bachelor of Arts from the University of Georgia and a Master of Business Administration (MBA) from the University of Miami School of Business, he has earned the Chartered Life Underwriter (CLU) and Chartered Financial Consultant (ChFC) designation. Mr. Rosenberg volunteers his time with Sea Turtle Rescue Operations, Nature Conservancy, and local beach and pier cleanups, as well as diving assistance for wounded veterans. He is passionate about his kids, the environment, and Ocean Photography.

www.rosenbergwealthmanagement.com

dannyonthebeach
Ocean Photography

(IG: dannyonthebeach)

Birth

Shore-break

Popoyo Mermaid

Board Games

Dragon Curl at Pompano

Phat Dragon Curl

Dawn Patrol at Maria's

Dragons Claw

Underwater Barrel at Trespass

Dragon Curl on The Playground

www.ingramcontent.com/pod-product-compliance
Lightning Source LLC
Chambersburg PA
CBHW071234130726
47998CB00003B/943